Five Marks of a Methodist

The Fruit of a Living Faith

Leader Guide
also includes Participant Character Guide

Magrey R. deVega
with Steve Harper

Abingdon Press

Nashville

FIVE MARKS OF A METHODIST LEADER GUIDE
Copyright © 2016 by Abingdon Press

This book is printed on acid-free paper.

978-1-5018-2024-3

Scripture quotations are from the Common English Bible. Copyright © 2011 by the Common English Bible. All rights reserved. Used by permission. www.CommonEnglishBible.com.

Hymn lyrics unless noted otherwise are taken from *The United Methodist Hymnal* (Nashville: The United Methodist Publishing House, 1989).

Hymn lyrics on page 56 are taken from http://www.hymntime.com/tch/htm/s/d/o/sdowarel.htm.

16 17 18 19 20 21 22 23 24 25—10 9 8 7 6 5 4 3 2 1
MANUFACTURED IN THE UNITED STATES OF AMERICA

Contents

How to Use This Leader Guide

Welcome to *Five Marks of a Methodist!* As a facilitator, you play a key role in the weekly classroom sessions, which are a critical component of the study's overall experience. Your guidance will shape the interactions between the participants and nurture the impact that this study has on their lives.

THE GOAL AND SCOPE OF *FIVE MARKS OF A METHODIST*

This study will guide your participants in a discovery of the essential qualities of United Methodist character, based on Dr. Steve Harper's book called *Five Marks of a Methodist: The Fruit of a Living Faith*. He provides an in depth study of John Wesley's treatise titled *The Character of a Methodist*, which describes the five marks of Methodist character:

1. A Methodist Loves God

2. A Methodist Rejoices in God

3. A Methodist Gives Thanks

4. A Methodist Prays Constantly

5. A Methodist Loves Others

This is a six-week study that begins with a general overview of Christian character, which Wesley believed to be the foundation of the spiritual life. Each of the following five weeks investigates one of the marks more fully. By the end of this study, your participants will be able to:

- Articulate the five essential marks of Methodist character;
- Ground their understanding of the five marks in the Bible and Wesleyan theology;
- Identify common barriers to living out each of the five marks;
- Renew their commitment to practicing the five marks in service to others for the glory of God.

THE ROLE OF FACILATOR

You do not have to be a formally trained Wesleyan scholar with profound biblical understanding in order to succeed as a facilitator. You need only the following attributes to do your work well:

Be a Learner: You are, first and foremost, a fellow participant on this journey. As you read the weekly material, you will be tempted to do so exclusively through the lens of a facilitator. Instead, allow yourself to be as transformed and inspired by these historic writings as you hope your participants will be. Cultivate a curiosity and openness to meanings that are important to you, and others will draw from your enthusiasm.

Be a Tour Guide: You do not need to be a resident expert on every biblical and theological matter that your group will discuss. Instead, like a docent in a museum, your job will simply be to direct their attention to aspects of our Wesleyan heritage and the Christian faith that are important for them to notice. You will guide conversations with structured questions designed to draw their interest and elicit their input.

Be Prepared: The success of the classroom experience is directly related to your level of preparedness before each session. Using the material in this leader guide, familiarize yourself with the learning objectives and key concepts for each week, carefully craft the questions that will spur conversation in your group, and structure both the time and the setting to be most conducive to learning.

Be Attentive to Stories: There is an easy tendency in a small group study like this one to get completely caught up in academic conversations about theology and biblical interpretation. Sometimes, however, the most effective way to deepen our understanding is through storytelling. Allow and encourage people to tell their own stories, modeling for them the power of storytelling by being vulnerable enough to do so yourself. Remember that a key to your group's success will be training people to listen to stories: not just the stories they share with others, but the grand, unfolding story of God's love found in scripture.

THE CLASSROOM EXPERIENCE

Each *Five Marks of a Methodist* session follows the same essential structure, with a suggested classroom length of 90 minutes:

GATHERING TOGETHER (5 minutes)

The opening questions of this segment are based on a unison reading of a passage in the book and help focus the group on the general theme of the session ahead.

REFLECTIONS ON THE READING (10 minutes)

This segment helps participants dig deeply into the central theme of the session by sharing discoveries from the reading and investigating key concepts together. Participation is often structured in pairs or small groups, in order to maximize sharing and encourage discussion from those who may be initially reluctant to do so.

VIDEO SEGMENT (15 minutes)

The video features Dr. Steve Harper, a retired professor of Spiritual Formation and Wesley Studies, and author of *Five Marks of a Methodist*. Participants will be able to gain wisdom from his personal reflections on the weekly theme, prompting their own ideas and questions.

VIDEO DISCUSSION QUESTIONS (10 minutes)

These questions prompt the participants to reflect on Dr. Harper's words in the context of their own discoveries.

REFLECTIONS ON THE SCRIPTURE (10 minutes)

Participants will explore the biblical foundations for each of the five marks by analyzing key scriptures included in the weekly reading. The questions in this leader guide will encourage a view of these scriptures that will connect the Bible to the main theme of the week, and will teach participants how to "go deeper" in the way they explore the Bible's meaning.

PRACTICAL APPLICATION (5 minutes)

Participants are encouraged to conceive and share tangible ways that this week's readings will alter their priorities and perspectives, and shape their behavior.

LOOKING AHEAD AND CLOSING PRAYER (5 minutes)

The appendix of this leader guide contains a participant character guide that will help persons in your group prepare for the next class. This is available in book and electronic form at Cokesbury.com. Encourage participants to prepare for the next week by following the daily readings and exercises that will introduce them to a wide array of resources from our Wesleyan heritage.

Each session then closes with a time for the sharing of prayer requests and concerns. Encourage participants to write down each other's needs and remember them in the upcoming week.

THE BASIC NEEDS OF A SMALL GROUP

Everyone has essential needs that emerge from three categories. To ensure a fruitful, healthy classroom experience for your participants, pay attention to these basic necessities:

PHYSICAL NEEDS: "Am I Safe and Comfortable?"

People have fundamental physical needs that must be addressed in order for them to maintain focus and attention. To meet these needs, ensure the following:

- Temperature: Set the thermostat in the room at a comfortable level.

- Comfort: Allow food, drinks, bathroom breaks, and time to stand up and stretch.

- Punctuality: Honor the time commitments people are making to the study by starting and ending each session promptly. When time is up, even if it is in the middle of a conversation, give people permission to leave if they need to, being particularly attentive to child care needs and nursery volunteers.

- Minimal Distractions: Reduce distracting outside noises. Invite people to silence their cell phones at the start of each session and to refrain from texting.

EMOTIONAL NEEDS: "Who Is Around Me? Can I Trust Them?"

For people to feel fully secure, they need to be comfortable with those around them. To meet these needs, ensure the following:

- Names: Learn people's names right away, say it to them often, and welcome them personally when they arrive.

9

- Chairs: Arrange the chairs in the room to suggest equality: no chairs higher, more comfortable, or more prominently placed than others.

- Prayer: Pray for your participants, even (and especially) before they meet for the first time. Always allow time for the sharing of joys and concerns at the conclusion of each session, and encourage people to share the task of offering the closing prayer.

- Confidentiality: Remind people often that what is shared during each session must remain kept to themselves.

- Healthy Disagreement: It is likely that people will offer contradictory points of view. Don't shy away from conflict, as sometimes those discussions will elicit opportunities for growth. However, don't let those disagreements become personal.

MENTAL NEEDS: *"Why Am I Here? What's the Point?"*

Finally, people need to know that the time they invest into this experience will be well spent. To be certain they can gauge the merits and progress of this process, ensure the following:

- Main Point: Share with the group the main points of each session that will direct their time and energies.

- Preparation: Model for them the benefits of being prepared by reading all the material in advance and keeping the discussions moving forward.

- Questions: Carefully construct the questions you will ask the group to discuss, tailored to the interests and dynamics of the group. Use "open-ended" questions that require more than simple responses from participants.

- Listen: Though you are a participant and are free to offer your own insights, model healthy conversation by being a good listener. The ideal ratio of talking/listening for a facilitator is 20/80.

10

- Enthusiasm: Share your excitement and encourage participation by completing all the assigned work yourself.

HELPFUL HINTS

Because every group is composed of different people, your class may have its own particular set of dynamics and challenges. The following are some tips to help your group succeed:

The ideal class size. Groups of eight to twelve people are an ideal size. Classes that are larger than twelve make it too easy for people to feel anonymous and even miss classes without being noticed. Large groups often take longer to form the kinds of relationships that are critical to meaningful small group study. Groups smaller than eight can lack the kind of diversity of background and opinion that enhance the richness of the experience.

What to do when a participant talks too much. When you sense that someone is commanding too much of the discussion, carefully determine whether or not that person is being a detriment to the group process. Some people, after all, have a personality that necessitates speaking in order to think. But if you discern that correction is necessary for the benefit of the class, first try some nonverbal cues. Avoid making eye contact with that person when you ask a question of the group. Break the group into smaller discussion groups in order to minimize the person's effect on the whole group. Also try some verbal cues: remind people after you ask certain questions to keep answers brief. Ask other people in the group for their response. Of course, if necessary, address the concern privately with an individual outside of class, thanking them for their contributions and asking for their assistance in eliciting discussion from others in the group.

What to do when a participant talks too little. There are individuals that require time to process their own thoughts before they verbalize them. Others are more introverted, shying away from talking in front of a large group. Again, manage eye contact to look directly at those who appear reluctant to talk. Breaking the group into pairs encourages everyone to share their opinions. Do refrain, however, from putting people on the spot. No one should feel coerced into speaking when they are uncomfortable. And when quieter people do choose to speak their thoughts in front of the whole group, praise them for their contribution without sounding patronizing.

Don't be afraid of silence. Sometimes, when you ask a question, there will be prolonged periods of silence in the group. You will be tempted to interrupt that silence with your own answers and insights, move quickly to another question, or call out people directly for their response. Instead, feel free to sit in that silence, trusting that people are sorting out their own answers and struggling in a healthy way. Rather than breaking that silence with your own answers, a good alternative is to break the class into smaller groups to discuss the question, making it less threatening for folks to develop their own responses verbally.

Stay on track. Inevitably, topics of conversation will emerge from your group that are not central to the main points of the session. Use your best judgment in discerning which discussions are more diversionary and less helpful. Gently return the conversation to the central ideas, and if need be, offer opportunities for interested folks to continue those conversations after class.

EPISODE 1

Character:
The Marks of a Methodist

INTRODUCTION

Character describes not just the qualities of an individual person; it is the foundation upon which a group of similarly characterized people discover and sustain their corporate meaning. In other words, the choices one makes about how one will live not only impact their own lives but also the lives of those with whom that person chooses to identify. And the opposite is also true: the corporate character of a group of people will also shape the individual choices that its members make. Group character both feeds and is fed by the choices of its participants.

This is the reason Wesley wrote his treatise *The Character of a Methodist*, which is the subject of our small group study. This opening session will help your class:

1. Explore the concept of "character" and why it is a foundational topic for spiritual growth;

2. Offer initial impressions of the five marks of a Methodist as a baseline for understanding;

3. Commit together to create an environment of support, prayer, and trust.

GATHERING (5 Minutes)

Invite participants to listen as you read aloud the following words of Charles Wesley's poem "Where Shall My Wondering Soul Begin": "Where shall my wondering soul begin? / How shall I all to heaven aspire? / A slave redeemed from death and sin, / A brand plucked from eternal fire, /how shall I equal triumphs raise, / and sing my great deliverer's praise?"

Invite students to reflect silently on those words for two minutes. After the silence, have them turn to a person next to them to share what words, phrases, or ideas resonate with them.

Ask a participant to open the session with a word of prayer.

REFLECTIONS ON THE READING (10 Minutes)

Have the class brainstorm a list of the kinds of groups they are involved in outside the church. That list might include civic organizations, service clubs, recreational sports leagues, work teams, etc. After the class has come up with that list, have them pair up and explore more deeply one of the groups on the list. For that group, have the pair write up a list of character qualities that can be used to describe not only the group as a whole but also the required characteristics of each member of the group. For example, for a sports team, character qualities might include "commitment to practice" and "desire to win." For a work team, qualities might include "trust in each other" and "dedication to the task."

Invite some of the pairs to share their conclusions. Then as a class, have everyone reflect on the question, "How does being part of a group shape the character qualities of individual members of that group?" Then, make the connection to the Christian church. Tell the class that for Methodists, there are five marks that define all people who call themselves Methodist. It is a list of expectations that every Methodist must fulfill as members of that group.

14

They are:

1. A Methodist Loves God

2. A Methodist Rejoices in God

3. A Methodist Gives Thanks

4. A Methodist Prays Constantly

5. A Methodist Loves Others

VIDEO SEGMENT (15 Minutes)

Video segment by Dr. Steve Harper, author of *Five Marks of a Methodist* and retired professor of Spiritual Formation and Wesley Studies.

VIDEO DISCUSSION QUESTIONS
(10 Minutes)

1. Do you agree that the culture (Wesley's and ours) determines value or worth by achievements and appearances (vs. character and integrity)? Why or why not?

2. Steve describes his father as a person of character. If character is how you act when no one is watching, who is a person of character in your corner of the world? Why?

3. What does it mean to say that in matters of the spiritual life we are always beginners? How will you begin again in the coming weeks?

THE JOURNEY AHEAD (15 Minutes)

A. The Five Marks

Have the class refer again to the list of five marks of a Methodist that will guide these sessions ahead. As a group, discuss each of the five marks, and ask people to share their understanding of what that mark means.

- What does it mean, for example, to rejoice in God?
- Of all the qualities that Wesley might have chosen, why is this one of the five that he identifies as important?
- What questions do you have about what this mark means?

B. The Character of This Group

Together, come up with a list of characteristics that will define this group's time together. What can they expect from each other in relation to each of the following characteristics:

- Being prepared for each session;
- Listening and contributing to each session;
- Honoring differences;
- Resolving conflict;
- Encouraging honesty and protecting confidentiality;
- Praying for each other;
- Being punctual and honoring each other's time;
- Creating an atmosphere of joy, love, and laughter.

After the class has come up with these shared values, have the list printed and displayed for all future sessions. Class members might even choose to sign the list to ritually commit to sharing those values.

LOOKING AHEAD AND CLOSING PRAYER
(5 Minutes)

Remind participants to keep up with the daily readings and exercises for the week ahead if they are using the participant character resource found in the appendix of this leader guide.

Have the class share joys and prayer concerns, and invite them to be in prayer for each other over the upcoming week. Invite someone to close in prayer.

The First Mark: A Methodist Loves God

INTRODUCTION

Loving God is part of the greatest commandment of Jesus, and it is a hallmark of the Methodist spiritual life. All of the other marks of a Methodist are drawn out of this central aspect of Christian character. Without loving God, the others are impossible to perform.

This session will help your class:

1. Determine how all that we love in our lives can flow out of our love for God;

2. Learn how to love God selflessly, rather than out of selfish motivation;

3. Discover how to love God with all our heart, being, and mind.

GATHERING (5 Minutes)

Invite participants to read in unison the quote from John Wesley at the beginning of chapter 1 of *Five Marks of a Methodist* (p. 1): "'What then is the mark? Who is a Methodist, according to your own account?'

I answer: A Methodist is one who has 'the love of God shed abroad in the heart by the Holy Ghost given to us.'" Invite students to reflect silently on those words for two minutes. After the silence, have them turn to a person next to them to share what words, phrases, or ideas resonate with them.

Ask a participant to open the session with a word of prayer.

REFLECTIONS ON THE READING
(10 Minutes)

Tell participants that Dr. Harper reminds us that to love God does not mean that we are not to love anything or anyone else, but that all of the love we share must flow out of the context of our love for God (p. 4).

Even though God's love is perfect, our human capacity to love is not. We are therefore prone to loving God out of purely self-seeking motivations, which is often expressed in prayers that are more about what God is doing for us, rather than simply acknowledging who God is.

Invite the class to work together on coming up with a list of qualities they believe describe God, ensuring that each quality is not about what God does for humans but simply describes who God is. For example, guide the class to think about descriptors such as "holy" and "just" and "mysterious" rather than "saving" and "comforting" and "always there when I need God."

Ask, "Was it difficult to come up with words that talk about God, apart from what God does for us? How might this list we came up with guide the way you love God simply for who God is?"

VIDEO SEGMENT (15 Minutes)

Video segment by Dr. Steve Harper, author of *Five Marks of a Methodist,* and retired professor of Spiritual Formation and Wesley Studies.

VIDEO DISCUSSION QUESTIONS
(10 Minutes)

1. Did your experience of God's love begin with someone who loved you or with the church and its story of God's saving love in the Bible (or somewhere else)?

2. Steve (and Wesley) remind us that God loves first and our love always follows that initiative. Share a time when you loved first and someone else responded.

3. Are you carrying a "thimble" or a "barrel" into the downpour of God's love this week? What would help you rightsize to a bigger vessel?

REFLECTIONS ON THE SCRIPTURE
(10 Minutes)

Invite someone in the class to read aloud Matthew 22:36-38. Have the class break up into three groups, and have them fill out one of the following three lists:

1. Ways to love God with all my heart

2. Ways to love God with all my being

3. Ways to love God with all my mind

After the groups have shared their lists with the class, have the class reflect together on barriers that prevent us from loving God in each of the ways described in those lists. Which ways are the most challenging? What barriers are the most difficult to overcome?

Next, have someone in the class read Romans 8:35-39. Have the class work together to make a list of all the barriers that might prevent us from God's love (notice in particular the words listed in verses 35, 38, and 39). Ask the class to reflect together on the question, "If God has broken down each of these barriers, what difference should that make in how we love God?"

PRACTICAL APPLICATION (5 Minutes)

Dr. Harper reminds us that the outcome of loving God is joy. Have someone read aloud the closing paragraph on p. 10, beginning with "As we can see from Wesley's exclamation above, the love of God produces joy." Then invite the class to break into groups of three and have them share with their partners the ways that they will choose to love God more this week and live a life of joy.

LOOKING AHEAD AND CLOSING PRAYER (5 Minutes)

Remind participants to keep up with the daily readings and exercises for the week ahead if they are using the participant character resource found in the appendix of this leader guide.

Have the class share joys and prayer concerns, and invite them to be in prayer for each other over the upcoming week. Invite someone to close in prayer.

The Second Mark: A Methodist Rejoices in God

INTRODUCTION

Joy is an essential ingredient to Christian character. It is not a fleeting emotion, such as happiness or gladness; nor is it always a conscious choice, such as contentment or patience. Rather, it is a result of one's encounter with the faithful love and grace of God. In other words, it is a natural response to the favor that God has given us, regardless of our circumstances.

This session will help your class:

1. Discover a fuller definition of biblical joy;

2. Identify the barriers that prevent us from experiencing joy;

3. Determine steps to have a freer experience of God's joy in our heads and hearts.

GATHERING (5 Minutes)

Invite participants to read in unison the lyrics from the Charles Wesley hymn "Rejoice the Lord Is King!" on page 20. "Rejoice the

Lord is King! / Your Lord and King adore; / mortals, give thanks and sing, / and triumph ever more. / Lift up your heart, lift up your voice; / rejoice; again I say, rejoice." Invite students to reflect silently on those words for two minutes. After the silence, have them turn to a person next to them to share what words, phrases, or ideas resonate with them.

Ask a participant to open the session with a word of prayer.

REFLECTIONS ON THE READING
(10 Minutes)

Invite participants to break into groups of three and describe for their partners a time when they experienced real joy. How was that feeling of joy similar to and different from happiness? Is there a difference?

Invite the class to break up into three groups, and have each group reflect together on one of the following quotes by Dr. Harper in this chapter:

- "The primary expression of strength is joy." (p. 16)

- "'Happiness' is a deeply ethical word that means the harvest of a life given over to righteousness." (p. 17)

- "The basis for our joy...is the atonement." (p. 19)

Ask each group to describe the meaning of these statements, perhaps restating the meaning in their own words. Then have each group share their explanations with the other two.

When all the groups have shared, ask the whole class to reflect together on these questions:

- "What are the obstacles that often prevent us from rejoicing in God in this way, and experiencing this kind of joy?"

- "What can we do to overcome these obstacles?"

VIDEO SEGMENT (15 Minutes)

Video segment by Dr. Steve Harper, author of *Five Marks of a Methodist*, and retired professor of Spiritual Formation and Wesley Studies.

VIDEO DISCUSSION QUESTIONS
(10 Minutes)

1. Wesley had no use for "dour godliness" and calls it "the Devil's religion." Who is the most joyous person you know? Describe that person.

2. How is joy the sign that we've experienced love? Is that true in your life?

3. What "joy set before you" kept you going through difficult times or "crosses" in your own life?

REFLECTIONS ON THE SCRIPTURE
(10 Minutes)

Break the class into four groups, and have each group reflect together on one of the following four scripture passages referenced in this chapter:

- Nehemiah 8:10
- Matthew 5:8, 12
- 1 John 4:18
- Romans 5:8

Have someone in the group read the passage aloud. Then ask the group to work together to answer the question: "What do these verses tell us is the source of our joy?"

PRACTICAL APPLICATION (5 Minutes)

One of the hallmarks of Wesleyan thought is its balance between the head and the heart, between thinking and emotion. For Wesley, there is no reason to choose between the two, as both are necessary in experiencing and understanding the fullness of God's love. Dr. Harper closed this chapter with a conversation between John Wesley and August Spangenburg that underscores this balance.

Have someone read that closing story aloud (found on page 20). Then invite the participants to break up into pairs and reflect with their partners on ways they will seek to find balance between their head and their heart in their experience of God's love this week.

To spur some ideas for people, the following might be ways to emphasize the "head":

- Reading books on the spiritual life, theology, or biblical study;
- Having deep conversations with a spiritual friend;
- Engaging a line of biblical interpretation or theological perspective with which they might not entirely agree.

The following might be ways to engage the "heart":

- Spending time in nature and communing with God;
- Singing or reading the lyrics to Wesley hymns;
- Creating artwork, poetry, or dance in response to some theological concept.

Invite them to share their experiences in next week's class.

LOOKING AHEAD AND CLOSING PRAYER
(5 Minutes)

Remind participants to keep up with the daily readings and exercises for the week ahead if they are using the participant character resource found in the appendix of this leader guide.

Have the class share joys and prayer concerns, and invite them to be in prayer for each other over the upcoming week. Invite someone to close in prayer.

The Third Mark:
A Methodist Gives Thanks

INTRODUCTION

Children learn the value of saying "thank you" at an early age. It is a core quality of a polite, decent character. We write thank-you notes for gifts that others give us; we express gratitude when others do us a favor; we offer appreciation to others when they do a good job.

But how often do we forget to say "thank you" to God? Perhaps we are quick to acknowledge many of our obvious blessings: health, family, and provision. But what difference would it make in our level of gratitude to God if we saw all of life and all of our being as gifts from God?

This session will help your class:

1. Heighten our awareness of God's many blessings, every day of our lives;

2. Discover how gratitude to God is rooted in an acknowledgment of God's nature, rather than simply blessings to us;

3. Renew a commitment to faithfully express gratitude to God.

GATHERING (5 Minutes)

Invite participants to read in unison the quote from John Wesley on page 27: "God, *you* the great creator and sovereign Lord of heaven and earth, *you* the father of angels and *human beings*, you the giver of life and protector of all *your* creatures, mercifully accept this my morning sacrifice of praise and thanksgiving, which I desire to offer, with all humility, to your divine majesty." Invite students to reflect silently on those words for two minutes. After the silence, have them turn to a person next to them to share what words, phrases, or ideas resonate with them.

Ask a participant to open the session with a word of prayer.

REFLECTIONS ON THE READING
(10 Minutes)

Invite participants to break into pairs and reflect on the question, "How hard is it to give thanks in every situation?" Have them discuss the types of situations when it is most difficult to be grateful to God.

Have the class break into three groups, and assign each group one of the questions that John Wesley used to examine his state of gratitude every Saturday evening:

1. Have I allotted some time for thanking God for the blessings of the past week?

2. Have I, in order to be the more sensible of them, seriously and deliberately considered the several circumstances that attended them?

3. Have I considered each of them as an obligation to greater love, and consequently, to stricter holiness?

Invite each group to define for themselves the meaning of each question, perhaps putting the question in their own words. Have them answer the question, "Why is this question important for cultivating an authentic and sincere attitude of thanksgiving?"

Have each group report their decisions and discoveries to the whole class. Then have the class discuss as a whole group the following question: "What difference might it make in our lives if we were to conscientiously answer these questions at least once a week, like John Wesley did?"

VIDEO SEGMENT (15 Minutes)

Video segment by Dr. Steve Harper, author of *Five Marks of a Methodist*, and retired professor of Spiritual Formation and Wesley Studies.

VIDEO DISCUSSION QUESTIONS (5 Minutes)

1. What are some concrete ways to develop a gratitude "antenna"? How does this remind you of God's grace in your life?

2. Think about Wesley's "recollection day" (Saturday) for remembering God's blessings that week. Would that work for you?

3. Offer a real-life example of giving thanks "in everything." When has that been difficult for you or someone you know?

REFLECTIONS ON THE SCRIPTURE (10 Minutes)

Break the class into four groups, and have each group reflect together on one of the following four scripture passages referenced in this chapter:

- 1 Peter 5:7
- Philippians 4:11

- 1 Thessalonians 5:18
- 2 Corinthians 9:15

Have someone in the group read the passage aloud. Then ask the group to work together to answer the questions: "What do these verses tell us about the nature and practice of thanksgiving? What reasons does this scripture passage give us to be grateful?"

PRACTICAL APPLICATION (5 Minutes)

Gratitude is a choice. It is a conscientious effort to give thanks to God, independent of situations at hand. Invite someone in the class to read out loud Dr. Harper's final paragraph on page 32, which describes a person who is able to give thanks in the midst of adversity. Then have the class read in unison the text of the Wesley hymn at the bottom of the page.

Invite the participants to break up into pairs and reflect with their partners on ways they will seek to be more grateful to God this week.

LOOKING AHEAD AND CLOSING PRAYER (5 Minutes)

Remind participants to keep up with the daily readings and exercises for the week ahead if they are using the participant character resource found in the appendix of this leader guide.

Have the class share joys and prayer concerns, and invite them to be in prayer for each other over the upcoming week. Invite someone to close in prayer.

EPISODE 5

The Fourth Mark: A Methodist Prays Constantly

INTRODUCTION

Prayer is the life blood of the Christian life. It maintains our intimate connection with God and is much broader than simply asking God for blessings. In fact, our view of God plays a direct role in the way we pray. If we see God as merely a cosmic butler or vending machine, then our prayers will simply be full of requests, and we will be disappointed in God if we don't get what we ask for. But if we see God as a faithful companion with whom we are called to be in relationship, then we see prayer as both the fertile ground and the fuel for that relationship to blossom and grow.

This session will help your class:

1. Identify the ways and circumstances it feels natural for us to pray, and times when it is difficult;

2. Redefine our perspective on prayer, from focusing on our needs to focusing on God;

3. Determine ways to grow in the capacity and frequency of our prayer life.

GATHERING (5 Minutes)

Invite participants to read in unison the words of Charles Wesley on page 45: "Pray, without ceasing pray / (Your Captain gives the word), / His summons cheerfully obey, / And call upon the Lord; / To God your every want / In instant prayer display; / Pray always; pray and never faint; / Pray, without ceasing pray." Invite students to reflect silently on those words for two minutes. After the silence, have them turn to a person next to them to share what words, phrases, or ideas resonate with them.

Ask a participant to open the session with a word of prayer.

REFLECTIONS ON THE READING
(10 Minutes)

Invite participants to break into pairs and reflect on the statement by Dr. Harper at the beginning of the chapter: "Discipleship is first and foremost a relationship between Jesus and us." Have them discuss how that changes their perception of spiritual growth, from perhaps simply being about commitment to the church, a sense of obligation, or force of habit. "Does it make a difference to you to see your spiritual life as primarily being about growing into a closer relationship with Jesus?"

Have the class break into two groups, and have each small group write two lists. On the first list, write down the situations in which it feels natural to pray, and on the second list, the situations where it is difficult to pray. For example, the class might identify meal times, family gatherings, or bedtime as moments when it is easier to pray. On the other hand, they might identify praying in public or in the midst of personal doubt as times when it is hard to pray. Have the groups compare lists. Have the class discuss the question, "How reasonable is it to expect that we can fulfill Paul's commandment to 'pray without ceasing'?"

Have the class then write up two more lists. On the first list, write down the methods of prayer that seem most comfortable to the class, and on the other list, write down ways to pray that are more difficult to practice. For example, the class might identify silent and private prayer as an easier way to pray than prayers spoken aloud in front of a group. Or they might say that written liturgies are easier to say, or perhaps not as meaningful because of antiquated language. Have them discuss the questions: "How important is it that we learn to practice a wide variety of prayer styles, rather than the ones that feel comfortable to us? Do you think God expects us to pray in ways that are not natural to us? Why or why not?"

VIDEO SEGMENT (15 Minutes)

Video segment by Dr. Steve Harper, author of *Five Marks of a Methodist*, and retired professor of Spiritual Formation and Wesley Studies.

VIDEO DISCUSSION QUESTIONS
(10 Minutes)

1. What do you think Steve means by prayer as "inclining" your heart to God? How is this different from "constant chattering"?

2. Have you ever used a prayer book (or the Lord's Prayer)? How could the "parentheses" approach make room for the real world that needs prayer?

3. What works best in your own prayer life? What are some strategies for making every moment a God-moment?

REFLECTIONS ON THE SCRIPTURE
(10 Minutes)

Break the class into four groups, and have each group reflect together on one of the four scripture passages related to prayer in this chapter:

- John 15:15
- Luke 11:1-13
- Luke 18:1-8
- Philippians 4:4-7

Have someone in the group read the passage aloud. Then ask the group to work together to answer the questions: "What do these verses tell us about the nature and practice of prayer? What reasons does this scripture passage give us to pray?"

PRACTICAL APPLICATION (5 Minutes)

Prayer ensures that our connection to God remains intimate and life-giving. Despite the many barriers that might interfere with a fully active prayer life, it is incumbent on Christians to stretch, grow both the capacity and frequency of our prayers. Invite someone in the class to read aloud the story of "Larry" on pages 42 and 43. Then invite members to turn to a partner and reflect on ways they will seek to grow in their prayer life this week.

PRAYER REQUESTS AND CLOSING PRAYER
(5 Minutes)

Remind participants to keep up with the daily readings and exercises for the week ahead if they are using the participant character resource found in the appendix of this leader guide.

Have the class share joys and prayer concerns, and invite them to be in prayer for each other over the upcoming week. Invite someone to close in prayer.

EPISODE 6

The Fifth Mark:
A Methodist Loves Others

INTRODUCTION

This final session is more than just the culmination of a series; it offers the fruition of all the previous marks of a Methodist. None of the prior marks matter if they do not in some way share the love of God with others. It reinforces what Dr. Harper calls our "vocational discipleship," which is both the motivation and the means of our spiritual life. All of our efforts and desire to grow closer to Jesus are not just for our own benefit but also for the benefit of those around us. Loving others is the fruit of a life faithfully lived.

This session will help your class:

1. Review each of the prior four marks and recast them in light of loving others;

2. Consider ways to make holiness a part of our daily living;

3. Explore ways to live out each of the five marks in daily life from now on.

GATHERING (5 Minutes)

Invite participants to read in unison the words of Charles Wesley on page 57: "Summoned my labor to renew, / And glad to act my part, /

35

Lord, in thy name my work I do, / And with a single heart." Invite students to reflect silently on those words for two minutes. After the silence, have them turn to a person next to them to share what words, phrases, or ideas resonate with them.

Ask a participant to open the session with a word of prayer.

REFLECTIONS ON THE READING
(10 Minutes)

Have the participants turn to a neighbor and share recollections of a person in their lives who embodied this mark of loving others. Who in their lives loved others with such consistency and grace that they were clearly doing so as a natural extension of their commitment to Jesus Christ? As part of their reflection, invite them to think of reasons it might be difficult for them to love others with that kind of regularity.

Have the class break into four groups, and have each small group work on completing the following sentences, based on the prior four marks of a Methodist:

- "We love God in order that _____."
- "We rejoice in God in order that _____."
- "We give thanks in order that _____."
- "We pray constantly in order that _____."

For each sentence completion, have the groups brainstorm ways that each mark of being a Methodist needs to contribute to some tangible way of loving others. In other words, how are each of these marks less about one's private relationship to God and more about the impact we can make on the lives of others?

VIDEO SEGMENT (15 Minutes)

Video segment by Dr. Steve Harper, author of *Five Marks of a Methodist*, and retired professor of Spiritual Formation and Wesley Studies.

VIDEO DISCUSSION QUESTIONS
(10 Minutes)

1. Can you recall anyone in your life who (like the cartoon character) "loves humanity" but seems to have little use for actual people? Have you ever felt that way? Why?

2. What are your everyday "fishing skills"? How can they be a part of the "vocational discipleship" that God's grace calls you to live?

3. Steve says, "This is doable." What will you do in the weeks ahead to make the five marks part of your daily walk with Jesus?

REFLECTIONS ON THE SCRIPTURE
(10 Minutes)

Break the class into four groups, and have each group reflect together on one of the following four scripture passages referenced in this chapter:

- 1 John 4:20
- Matthew 22:37-39
- Colossians 3:13
- Romans 12:1

Have someone in the group read the passage aloud. Then ask the group to work together to answer the questions: "What do these verses tell us about God's call for us to make a difference in the lives of others? What reasons does this scripture passage give us to love others?"

PRACTICAL APPLICATION (5 Minutes)

Invite someone in the class to read aloud Henri Nouwen's quotation on page 56. Remind them that the ultimate goal of the Christian life is not simply to ensure a place to go after we die, but to shape the very life we are living in the here and now. Have them turn to a partner and share what ways they will determine to live out each of the five marks in their lives from this moment on.

LOOKING AHEAD AND CLOSING PRAYER
(5 Minutes)

Remind your group that a real-world faith connects us to others and draws us into "360-degree discipleship" beyond our narrow identity groups: a disciple is a Christian in and with a world of others.

Have the class share joys and prayer concerns, and invite them to be in prayer for each other over the upcoming week. Invite someone to close in prayer.

Participant Character Guide

At the conclusion of each session, draw attention to the *Participant Character Guide*, which provides a daily exercise that prompts the reading of the next chapter and introduces the participant to a wide array of biblical and Wesleyan resources for the spiritual life.

The *Participant Character Guide* also provides ample space for participants to write their own reflections to the reading and the daily exercises, which will shape their participation in the weekly sessions.

The First Mark:
A Methodist Loves God

INTRODUCTION

Loving God is part of the greatest commandment of Jesus, and it is a hallmark of the Methodist spiritual life. All of the other marks of a Methodist are drawn out of this central aspect of Christian character; without loving God, the others are impossible to perform.

This session will help you and others in your class:

1. Determine how all that you love in your life can flow out of your love for God;

2. Learn how to love God selflessly, rather than out of selfish motivation;

3. Discover how to love God with all your heart, being, and mind.

DAY ONE: Chapter Reading

Read chapter 1 of *Five Marks of a Methodist*, pages 1–11, titled "A Methodist Loves God." Write your reflections on the reading here.

DAY TWO: *Scripture Reading*

Read Matthew 22:36-38 and Romans 8:35-39. Read each passage at a normal pace the first time, and then read each passage again slowly a second time, looking for words or phrases that catch your attention. Then, pause for silent prayer for a few minutes to listen for what the Spirit might be prompting you about these passages. Read the passages again for a third and final time, then write your reflections in the space below.

DAY THREE: *Wesley Hymn*

Read or sing the text of the following hymn by Charles Wesley, then write your reflections on the hymn in the space below.

"Love Divine, All Loves Excelling"

Love divine, all loves excelling,
joy of heaven, to earth come down,
fix in us thy humble dwelling;
all thy faithful mercies crown.
Jesus, thou art all compassion,
pure, unbounded love thou art;
visit us with thy salvation;
enter every trembling heart.

Breathe, O breathe thy loving Spirit
into every troubled breast!

Let us all in thee inherit;
let us find that second rest.
Take away our bent to sinning;
Alpha and Omega be;
end of faith, as its beginning,
set our hearts at liberty.

Come, Almighty to deliver,
let us all thy life receive;
suddenly return and never,
nevermore thy temples leave.
Thee we would be always blessing,
serve thee as thy hosts above,
pray and praise thee without ceasing,
glory in thy perfect love.

Finish, then, thy new creation;
pure and spotless let us be.
Let us see thy great salvation
perfectly restored in thee;
changed from glory into glory,
till in heaven we take our place,
till we cast our crowns before thee,
lost in wonder, love, and praise.

DAY FOUR: *Sermon by John Wesley*

Read John Wesley's sermon "The Marks of the New Birth" found online at http://www.umcmission.org/Find-Resources/John-Wesley -Sermons/Sermon-18-The-Marks-of-the-New-Birth. Write your reflections in the space below.

DAY FIVE: *Service*

Look for a practical way today to serve someone else using the lessons you have learned so far about loving God. Write what you did and your reflections in the space below.

DAY SIX: *Wesley's Questions*

In the early days of Methodism, John Wesley instructed each small group to answer certain questions aloud in the presence of others in the group, for the purpose of shared accountability and support. The following are two of the questions they asked of each other. Reflect on your answers in the space below.

Did the Bible live in me today?
Is Christ real to me?

The Second Mark:
A Methodist Rejoices in God

INTRODUCTION

Joy is an essential ingredient to Christian character. It is not a fleeting emotion, such as happiness or gladness; nor is it always a conscious choice, such as contentment or patience. Rather, it is a result of one's encounter with the faithful love and grace of God. In other words, it is a natural response to the favor that God has given us, regardless of our circumstances.

This session will help you and others in your class:

1. Discover a fuller definition of biblical joy;

2. Identify the barriers that prevent you from experiencing joy;

3. Determine steps to have a freer experience of God's joy in your head and heart.

DAY ONE: Chapter Reading

Read chapter 2 of *Five Marks of a Methodist*, pages 13–21, titled "A Methodist Rejoices in God." Write your reflections on the reading here.

DAY TWO: Scripture Reading

Read Nehemiah 8:10 and Matthew 5:8, 12. Read each passage at a normal pace the first time, and then read each passage again slowly a second time, looking for words or phrases that catch your attention. Then, pause for silent prayer for a few minutes to listen for what the Spirit might be prompting you about these passages. Read the passages again for a third and final time, then write your reflections in the space below.

DAY THREE: Wesley Hymn

Read or sing the text of the following hymn by Charles Wesley, then write your reflections on the hymn in the space below.

"Rejoice, The Lord Is King"

Rejoice, the Lord is King!
Your Lord and King adore;
mortals, give thanks and sing,
And triumph evermore.
Lift up your heart,
lift up your voice;
rejoice; again I say, rejoice.

Jesus the Savior reigns,
the God of truth and love;
when he had purged our stains,
he took his seat above.
Lift up your heart,

lift up your voice;
rejoice; again I say, rejoice.

His kingdom cannot fail;
he rules o'er earth and heaven;
the keys of earth and hell
are to our Jesus given.
Lift up your heart,
lift up your voice;
rejoice; again I say, rejoice.

Rejoice in glorious hope!
Jesus the Judge shall come,
and take his servants up
to their eternal home.
Lift up your heart,
lift up your voice;
rejoice; again I say, rejoice.

DAY FOUR: *Sermon by John Wesley*

Read John Wesley's sermon "The More Excellent Way" found online at http://www.umcmission.org/Find-Resources/John-Wesley-Sermons/Sermon-89-The-More-Excellent-Way. Write your reflections in the space below.

DAY FIVE: *Service*

Look for a practical way today to serve someone else using the lessons you have learned so far about rejoicing in God. Write what you did and your reflections in the space below.

DAY SIX: *Wesley's Questions*

In the early days of Methodism, John Wesley instructed each small group to answer certain questions aloud in the presence of others in the group, for the purpose of shared accountability and support. The following are two of the questions they asked of each other. Reflect on your answers in the space below.

Do I grumble or complain constantly?
Am I defeated in any part of my life?

The Third Mark:
A Methodist Gives Thanks

INTRODUCTION

Children learn the value of saying "thank you" at an early age. It is a core quality of a polite, decent character. We write thank-you notes for gifts that others give us; we express gratitude when others do us a favor; we offer appreciation to others when they do a good job.

But how often do we forget to say "thank you" to God? Perhaps we are quick to acknowledge many of our obvious blessings: health, family, and provision. But what difference would it make in our level of gratitude to God if we saw all of life and all of our being as gifts from God?

This session will help you and others in your class:

1. Heighten your awareness of God's many blessings, every day of your life;

2. Discover how gratitude to God is rooted in God's nature, rather than simply blessings to you;

3. Renew a commitment to faithfully express gratitude to God.

DAY ONE: Chapter Reading

Read chapter 3 of *Five Marks of a Methodist*, pages 23–33, titled "A Methodist Gives Thanks." Write your reflections on the reading here.

DAY TWO: Scripture Reading

Read 1 Peter 5:7 and Philippians 4:11. Read each passage at a normal pace the first time, and then read each passage again slowly a second time, looking for words or phrases that catch your attention. Then, pause for silent prayer for a few minutes to listen for what the Spirit might be prompting you about these passages. Read the passages again for a third and final time, then write your reflections in the space below.

DAY THREE: *Wesley Hymn*

Read or sing the text of the following hymn by Charles Wesley, then write your reflections on the hymn in the space below:

"O For a Thousand Tongues to Sing"

O for a thousand tongues to sing
my great Redeemer's praise,
the glories of my God and King,
the triumphs of his grace!

My gracious Master and my God,
assist me to proclaim,
to spread through all the earth abroad
the honors of thy name.

Jesus! the name that charms our fears,
that bids our sorrows cease;
'tis music in the sinner's ears,
'tis life, and health, and peace.

He breaks the power of canceled sin,
he sets the prisoner free;
his blood can make the foulest clean;
his blood availed for me.

DAY FOUR: Sermon by John Wesley

Read John Wesley's sermon "God's Love to Fallen Man" found online at http://www.umcmission.org/Find-Resources/John-Wesley-Sermons/Sermon-59-Gods-Love-to-Fallen-Man. Write your reflections in the space below.

DAY FIVE: Service

Look for a practical way today to serve someone else using the lessons you have learned so far about giving thanks. Write what you did and your reflections in the space below.

DAY SIX: Wesley's Questions

In the early days of Methodism, John Wesley instructed each small group to answer certain questions aloud in the presence of others in the group, for the purpose of shared accountability and support. The following are two of the questions they asked of each other. Reflect on your answers in the space below.

Am I jealous, impure, critical, irritable, touchy, or distrustful?
How do I spend my spare time?

The Fourth Mark:
A Methodist Prays Constantly

INTRODUCTION

Prayer is the life blood of the Christian life. It maintains our intimate connection with God and is much broader than simply asking God for blessings. In fact, our view of God plays a direct role in the way we pray. If see God as merely a cosmic butler or vending machine, then our prayers will simply be full of requests, and we will be disappointed in God if we don't get what we ask for. But if we see God as a faithful companion with whom we are called to be in relationship, then we see prayer as both the fertile ground and the fuel for that relationship to blossom and grow.

This session will help you and others in your class:

1. Identify the ways and circumstances that it feels natural for you to pray, and times when it is difficult;

2. Redefine your perspective on prayer, from focusing on your needs to focusing on God;

3. Determine ways to grow in the capacity and frequency of your prayer life.

DAY ONE: *Chapter Reading*

Read chapter 4 of *Five Marks of a Methodist*, pages 35–45, titled "A Methodist Prays Constantly." Write your reflections on the reading here.

DAY TWO: *Scripture Reading*

Read John 15 and Luke 11:1-13. Read each passage at a normal pace the first time, and then read each passage again slowly a second time, looking for words or phrases that catch your attention. Then, pause for silent prayer for a few minutes to listen for what the Spirit might be prompting you about these passages. Read the passages again for a third and final time, then write your reflections in the space below.

DAY THREE: Wesley Hymn

Read or sing the text of the following hymn by Charles Wesley, then write your reflections on the hymn in the space below.

"Shepherd Divine, Our Wants Relieve"

Shepherd divine, our wants relieve
In this our evil day,
To all Thy tempted followers give
The power to watch and pray.

Long as our fiery trials last,
Long as the cross we bear,
O let our souls on Thee be cast
In never ceasing prayer!

The Spirit of interceding grace
Give us in faith to claim;
To wrestle till we see Thy face,
And know Thy hidden name.

Till thou Thy perfect love impart,
Till thou thyself bestow,
Be this the cry of every heart,
"I will not let Thee go:

"I will not let Thee go, unless
Thou tell Thy name to me,
With all Thy great salvation bless,
And make me all like Thee:

Then let me on the mountain top
Behold Thy open face,
Where faith in sight is swallowed up,
And prayer in endless praise.

DAY FOUR: *Sermon by John Wesley*

Read John Wesley's sermon "The Important Question" found online at http://www.umcmission.org/Find-Resources/John-Wesley-Sermons/Sermon-84-The-Important-Question. Write your reflections in the space below.

DAY FIVE: *Service*

Look for a practical way today to serve someone else using the lessons you have learned so far about praying constantly. Write what you did and your reflections in the space below.

DAY SIX: *Wesley's Questions*

In the early days of Methodism, John Wesley instructed each small group to answer certain questions aloud in the presence of others in the group, for the purpose of shared accountability and support. The following are two of the questions they asked of each other. Reflect on your answers in the space below.

Am I enjoying prayer?
Do I pray about the money I spend?

The Fifth Mark:
A Methodist Loves Others

INTRODUCTION

This final session is more than just the culmination of a series; it offers the fruition of all the previous marks of a Methodist. None of the prior marks matter if they do not in some way share the love of God with others. It reinforces what Dr. Harper calls our "vocational discipleship," which is both the motivation and the means of our spiritual life. All of our efforts and desire to grow closer to Jesus are not just for our own benefit but also for the benefit of those around us. Loving others is the fruit of a life faithfully lived.

This session will help you and others in your class:

1. Review each of the prior four marks and recast them in light of loving others;

2. Consider ways to make holiness a part of your daily living;

3. Explore ways to live out each of the five marks in daily life from now on.

DAY ONE: *Chapter Reading*

Read chapter 5 of *Five Marks of a Methodist*, pages 47–57, titled "A Methodist Loves Others." Write your reflections on the reading here.

DAY TWO: *Scripture Reading*

Read 1 John 4:20 and Matthew 22:37-39. Read each passage at a normal pace the first time, and then read each passage again slowly a second time, looking for words or phrases that catch your attention. Then, pause for silent prayer for a few minutes to listen for what the Spirit might be prompting you about these passages. Read the passages again for a third and final time, then write your reflections in the space below.

DAY THREE: *Wesley Hymn*

Read or sing the text of the following hymn by Charles Wesley, then write your reflections on the hymn in the space below.

"A Charge to Keep I Have"

A charge to keep I have,
a God to glorify,
a never-dying soul to save,
and fit it for the sky.

To serve the present age,
my calling to fulfill;
O may it all my powers engage
to do my Master's will!

Arm me with jealous care,
as in thy sight to live,
and oh, thy servant, Lord, prepare
a strict account to give!

Help me to watch and pray,
and on thyself rely,
assured, if I my trust betray,
I shall forever die.

DAY FOUR: Sermon by John Wesley

Read John Wesley's sermon "On Love" found online at http://
www.umcmission.org/Find-Resources/John-Wesley-Sermons/Sermon
-139-On-Love. Write your reflections in the space below.

DAY FIVE: Service

Look for a practical way today to serve someone else using the lessons you have learned so far about loving others. Write what you did
and your reflections in the space below.

DAY SIX: *Wesley's Questions*

In the early days of Methodism, John Wesley instructed each small group to answer certain questions aloud in the presence of others in the group, for the purpose of shared accountability and support. The following are two of the questions they asked of each other. Reflect on your answers in the space below.

Is there anyone whom I fear, dislike, disown, criticize, hold a resentment toward, or disregard? If so, what am I doing about it?
When did I last speak to someone else about my faith?

CPSIA information can be obtained
at www.ICGtesting.com
Printed in the USA
LVOW01s0328140116
470545LV00003B/7/P